W9-CFJ-587

WITHDRAWN

North Plains Public Library
31360 NW Commercial Street
North Plains, OR 97133-6215

From NPPL

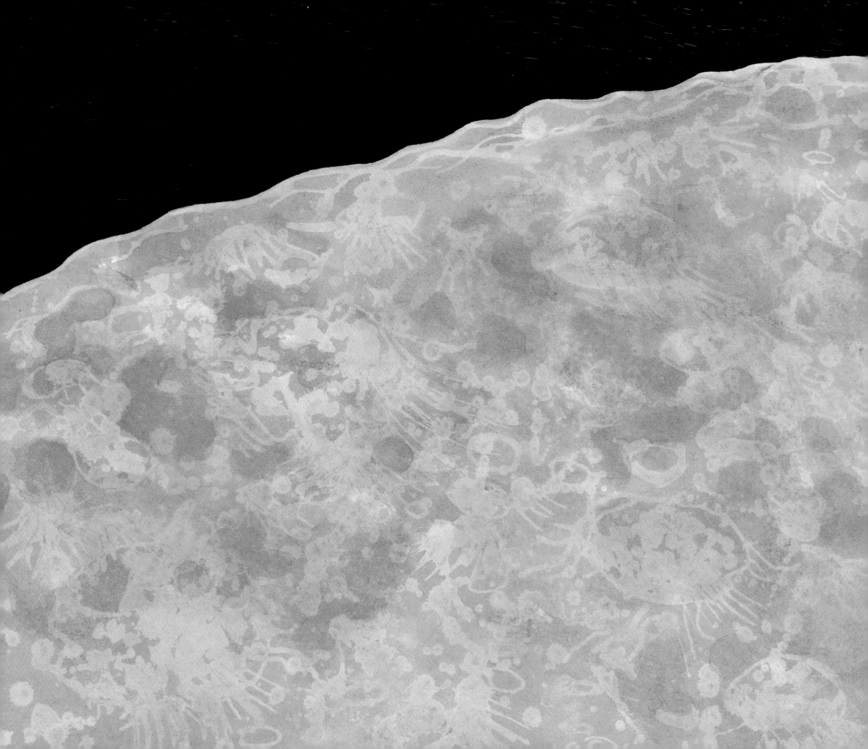

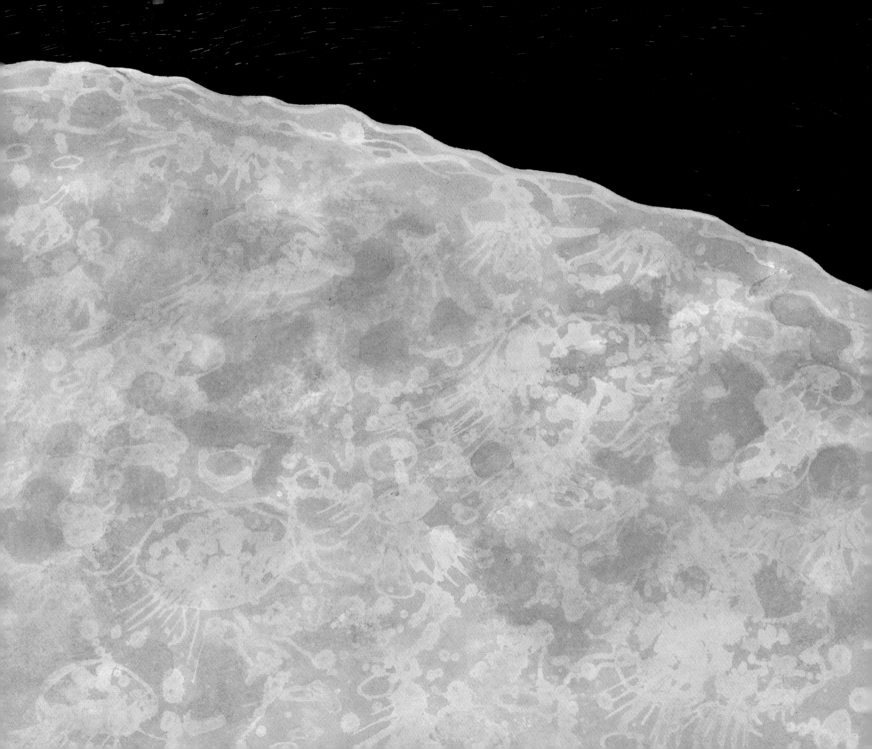

LET'S-READ-AND-FIND-OUT SCIENCE®

STAGE
2

What the Moon Is Like

by Franklyn M. Branley

illustrated by True Kelley

HarperCollinsPublishers

Special thanks to Amie Gallagher
at the American Museum–Hayden Planetarium for her expert advice.

To Michael Bridges and Amanda Bridges
—F.M.B.

To Steven Lindblom
—T.K.

The *Let's-Read-and-Find-Out Science* book series was originated by Dr. Franklyn M. Branley, Astronomer Emeritus and former Chairman of the American Museum–Hayden Planetarium, and was formerly co-edited by him and Dr. Roma Gans, Professor Emeritus of Childhood Education, Teachers College, Columbia University. Text and illustrations for each of the books in the series are checked for accuracy by an expert in the relevant field. For more information about Let's-Read-and-Find-Out Science books, write to HarperCollins Children's Books, 195 Broadway, New York, NY 10007.

HarperCollins®, ®, and Let's Read-and-Find-Out Science®
are trademarks of HarperCollins Publishers Inc.

What the Moon Is Like
Text copyright © 1963, 1986 by Franklyn M. Branley
Illustrations copyright © 2000 by True Kelley
All rights reserved. No part of this book may be used or reproduced in any manner whatsoever
without written permission except in the case of brief quotations embodied in critical articles and reviews.
Manufactured in China. For information address HarperCollins Children's Books,
a division of HarperCollins Publishers, 195 Broadway, New York, NY 10007.
http://www.harperchildrens.com

Library of Congress Cataloging-in-Publication Data
Branley, Franklyn Mansfield, 1915–
    What the moon is like / by Franklyn M. Branley ; illustrated by True Kelley. — Newly illustrated ed.
        p.   cm. — (Let's-read-and-find-out science.   Stage 2)
    Previously published: New York : Harper & Row, 1986.
    Summary: Imagines sights and experiences on a moon visit.
    ISBN 0-06-027992-3. — ISBN 0-06-027993-1 (lib. bdg.). — ISBN 0-06-445185-2 (pbk.)
    1. Moon—Juvenile literature.   [1. Moon.]   I. Kelley, True, ill.   II. Title.   III. Series.
QB582.B73   2000   98-54072
559.9'1—dc21   CIP
                                                                                                                   AC

Typography by Elynn Cohen
16 17 18 SCP 25 24 23 22
❖
Newly Illustrated Edition

The next time you see a big, round moon, look for the man in the moon. The dark and light parts make some people think of a mouth, a nose, and two eyes. That is why they say there is a man in the moon.
Can you see him?

Other people say there is a rabbit in the moon.

It has big ears.

Some people see Jack and Jill and their pail of water.

Maybe a cat sees a mouse in the moon.

Maybe a mouse sees a piece of cheese.

Next time you see the moon, look for the man, the rabbit, and Jack and Jill. You may be able to see them if you try real hard. Some people try hard but can't see any of them.

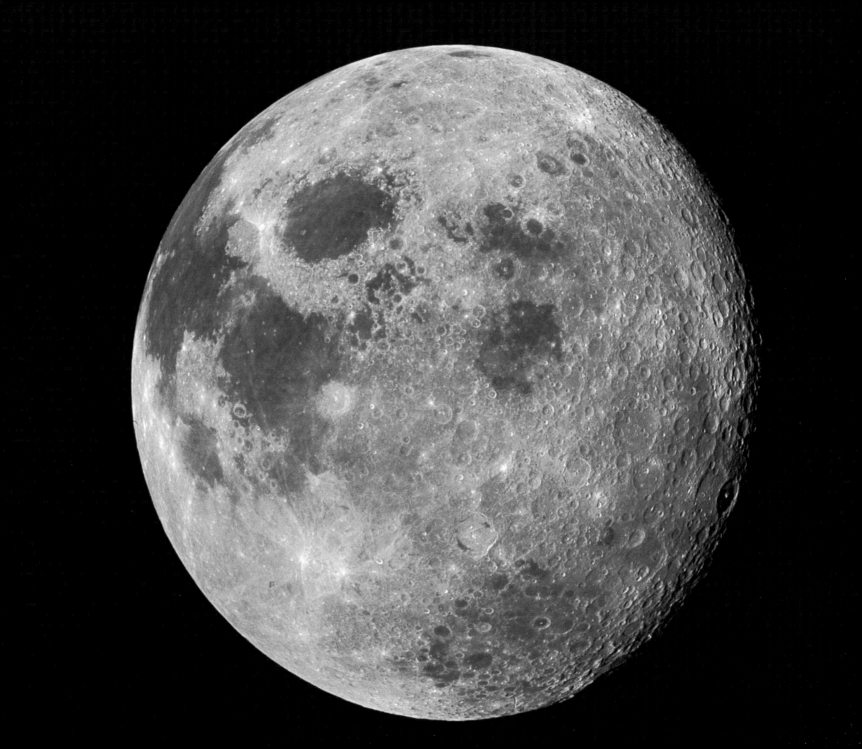

If you could see the moon better, it would look like this. The light parts are covered with hills, and with holes called craters. Some are many miles across. Others are very small. The holes were made by big rocks that crashed into the moon long ago.

The dark parts of the moon are smoother. They are like wide fields. It would take weeks to walk across some of them. They are called the seas of the moon because they are so flat. There is no water in them.

Twelve men have gone to the moon. Look at the map to see where they landed. They walked on the moon. Some of these astronauts rode in a moon car called a Lunar Roving Vehicle. The astronauts found no air on the moon. Outside their ship the men wore space suits. The air they needed was carried inside the suits.

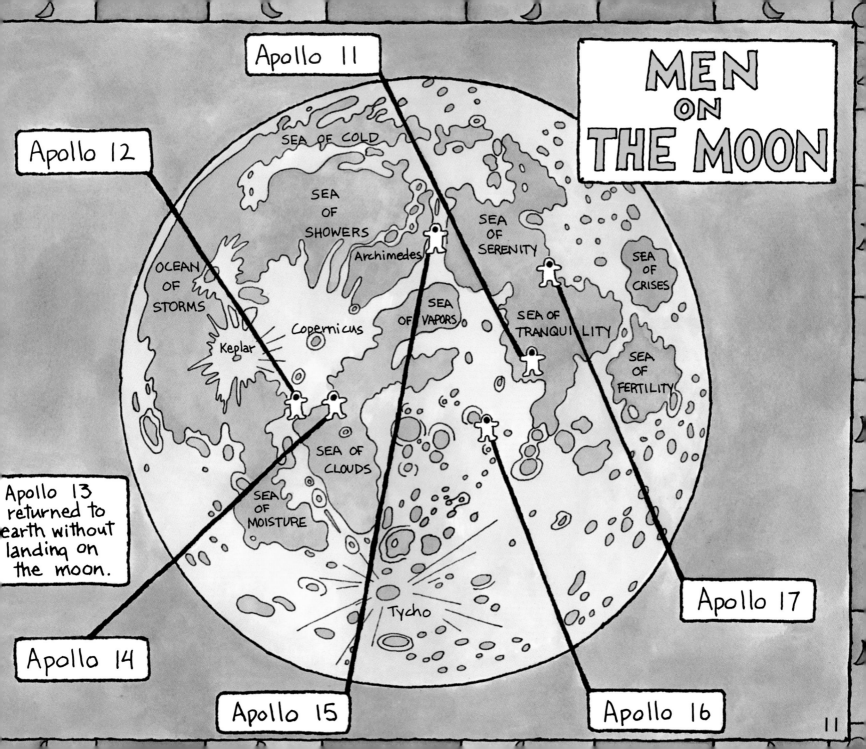

They found small rocks and great big ones. Some were as big as a house. Parts of the moon are flat. In those places the astronauts could move quite easily. But there are many mountains and hills. Some are smooth and rounded. Some have large jagged rocks sticking out of them. There are cliffs and deep valleys. The astronauts kept away from them.

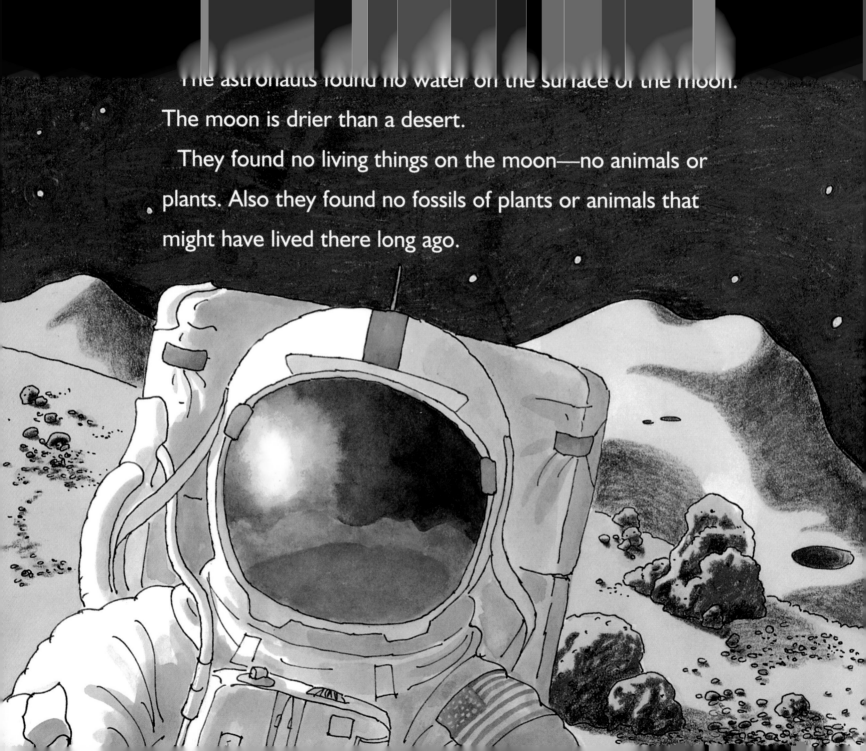

The astronauts found no water on the surface of the moon.
The moon is drier than a desert.
They found no living things on the moon—no animals or plants. Also they found no fossils of plants or animals that might have lived there long ago.

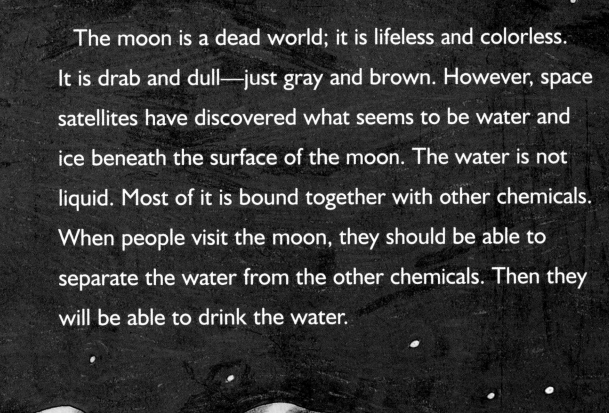

The moon is a dead world; it is lifeless and colorless. It is drab and dull—just gray and brown. However, space satellites have discovered what seems to be water and ice beneath the surface of the moon. The water is not liquid. Most of it is bound together with other chemicals. When people visit the moon, they should be able to separate the water from the other chemicals. Then they will be able to drink the water.

The moon has a long day and a long night. There are two weeks of daylight on the moon. Then there are two weeks of darkness.

In daytime the moon gets very hot. The temperature reaches 250 degrees Fahrenheit. That's hotter than boiling water. There is no air to protect the moon from the sun.

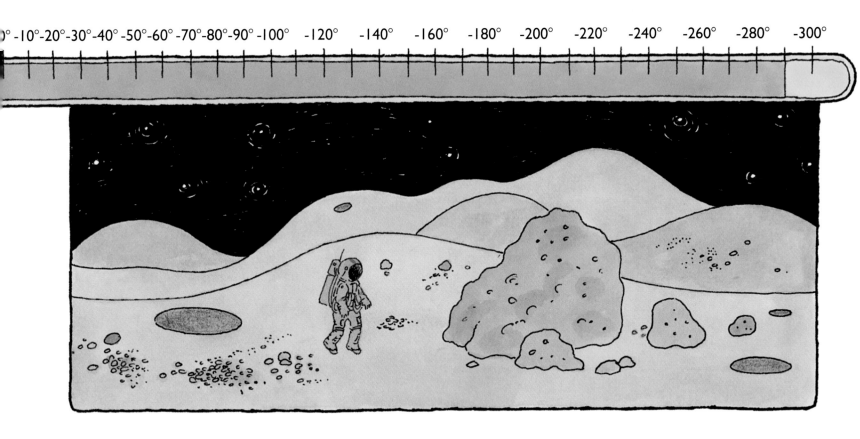

It is very cold in shadowed places behind big rocks. And at night the moon gets icy cold, about 290 degrees below zero. There is no air to hold the heat.

Space suits kept the astronauts from getting too hot in daytime and too cold at night or in shadows.

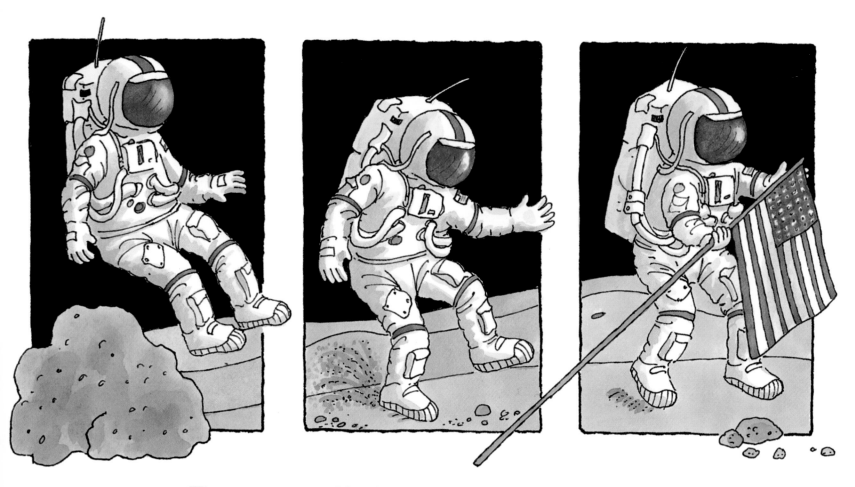

The astronauts liked walking on the moon. They did not weigh very much, because gravity on the moon is less than it is on Earth. They felt light. You would, too. If you weigh sixty pounds on Earth, you would weigh only ten pounds on the moon.

Because gravity on the moon is low, the astronauts could take giant steps. They bounded up and down. But their space suits were bulky and awkward. The astronauts had to be careful so they would not fall down.

If they did fall, it was hard for them to get up because of the clumsy space suits, and also because of the moon dust. Much of the moon is covered with fine dust, almost like powder. In many places the dust is a foot or more deep. When the astronauts walked, their boots made prints in the dust. The moon car had to have wide tires to keep from sinking into it. The dust stuck to their space suits, too.

The moon changes very little. It is almost the same today as it has been for billions of years. That's partly because nothing grows on the moon. Also, there are no rivers and streams to wear down the hills. And there is no wind to move dust from one place to another.

Earth is always changing. All kinds of plants and animals live here, and they keep changing Earth. Our planet also has water that wears down rocks. We also have wind that blows dust and dirt, moving it from place to place.

After Earth and the moon were formed, big rocks crashed into them. There were also a lot of volcanoes that spouted dust and ash. They spread hot liquid rock (or lava) over parts of Earth and the moon. On Earth much of the lava has been worn away. It is still unchanged on the moon.

Smaller rocks still crash into the moon. They also crash into Earth, but not very often.

On Earth our daytime sky is bright and blue. That's because water droplets, dust particles, and molecules in the air are lighted by the sun.

There is no air on the moon—no dust, water droplets, or molecules in the sky. There is nothing in the sky to be lighted, so it is always black.

From the moon, people can see the stars at night, just as we can from Earth. But they can see the stars in daytime, too. They can see stars in the black sky when the sun is shining.

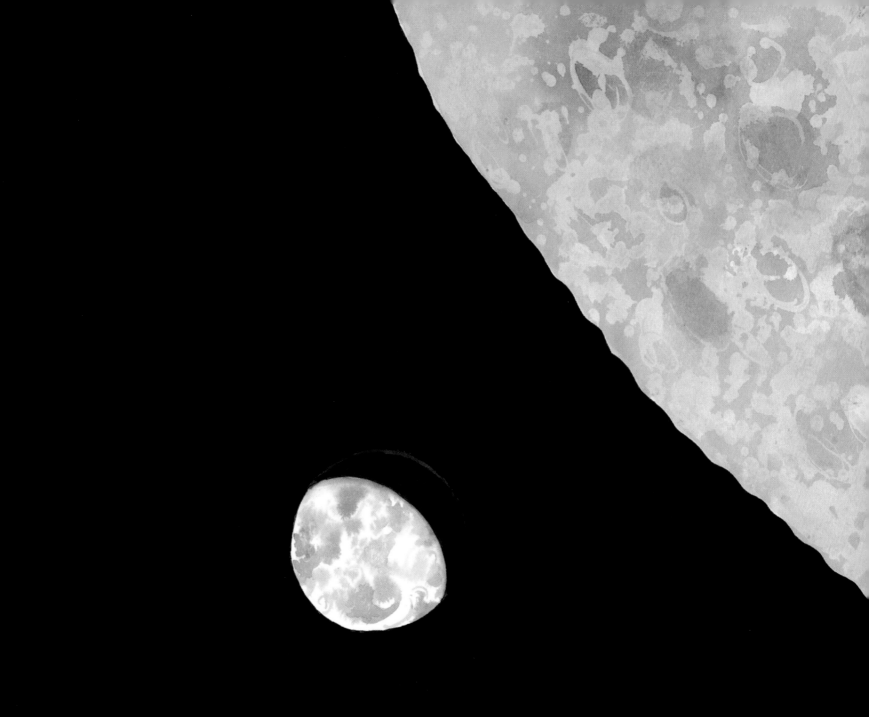

When the astronauts started for home, they could see the moon just below them. They could see Earth far in the distance.

Someday astronauts will probably go to the moon again. Once more they will explore it. They may put up buildings on the moon and live inside them. They may start a moon colony.

Who knows—someday you may work in a moon colony. You may be a moon explorer. Then you'll see for yourself what the moon is like.

FIND OUT MORE ABOUT THE MOON

- **M**ake a moon crater! You will need: an aluminum pie pan or a shallow plastic bowl, flour, cocoa powder, and a marble or pebble. Fill the pie pan or the bowl with flour, about two inches deep, and cover the flour with a thin layer of cocoa powder. Drop the marble or pebble into the flour from a height of four or five inches. What happens to the flour after you drop the marble or pebble is a lot like what happens to the moon's surface after it is hit by a meteor.

- **I**magine living in a moon colony. Draw a picture of what your house might look like, or keep a diary of what you might do every day for a week. What would you eat? Would you go to school? What would you do for fun?

- **H**ow much would you weigh on the moon? Find out how much you weigh in pounds. Then divide that number by six. That's how much you would weigh on the moon.

- **E**xplore these web sites to find out more about the moon and outer space:
    www.jsc.nasa.gov
    images.jsc.nasa.gov
    www.armagh-planetarium.co.uk/mirrors/nineplanets

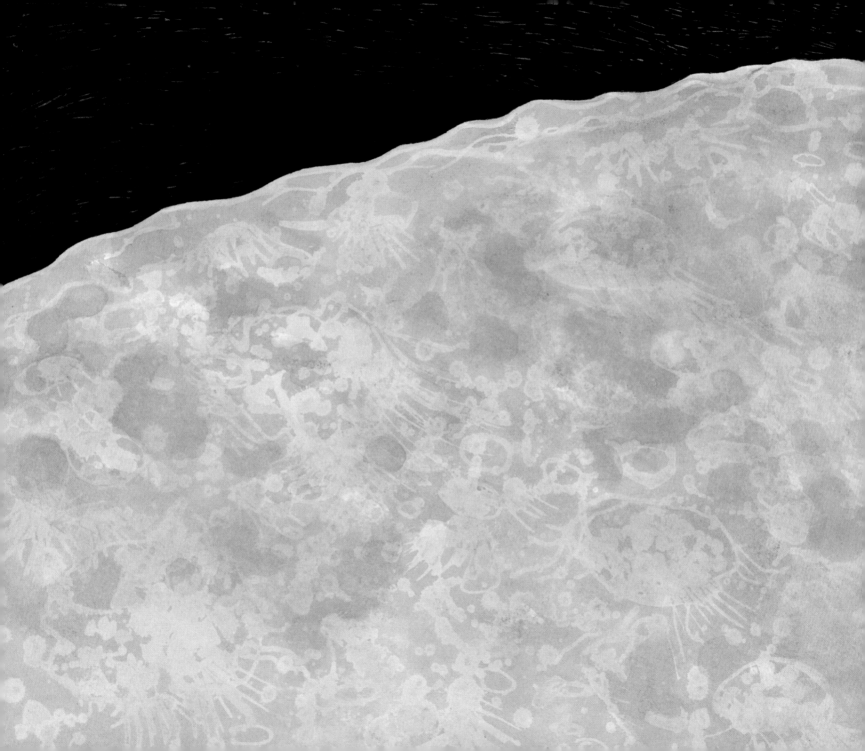

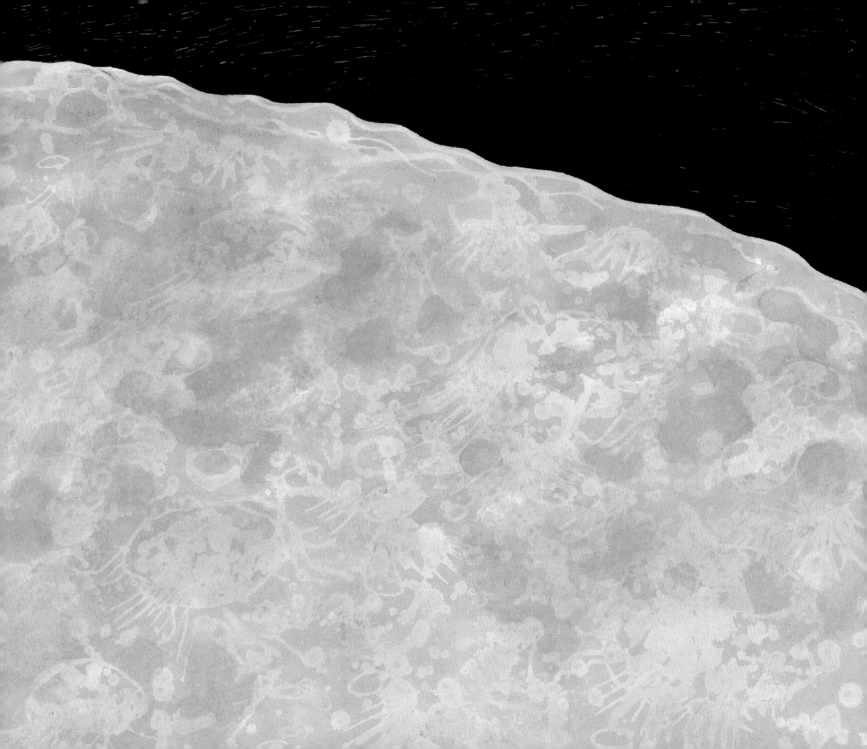

WITHDRAWN
From NPPL

North Plains Public Library
31360 NW Commercial Street
North Plains, OR 97133-6215